Start Up and Run Your Own Successful Wedding Planning Business -

A 'How To' Guide for Aspiring Wedding Planners.

Kerry Jackson-Rider.

Kerry Jackson-Rider.

Kerry Jackson-Rider.

DEDICATION.

Dedicated to and in loving memory of my mum, Jean Orman, (nee Clemons) 1941 - 2012. I miss you xx

CONTENTS.

FOREWORD
BY KERRY JACKSON-RIDER.

Hello Aspiring Wedding Planner and welcome to this 'How to' guide. I have been planning weddings around the world since 2010 in which time I have learned a lot about the wedding industry and what works well in both the process of wedding planning and in running a wedding planning business. I, like others before me, have learned most things the hard way by investing lots of time and money in research and continually learning mostly by trial and error.

So, that's the reason I want to help YOU learn how to start up and run your own successful Wedding Planning business without having to go through all of the trials and tribulations as I did. So let's just cut right to the chase with no bull and no fluff and just concentrate on the FACTS! I will use this hopefully user-friendly guide book to help my like-minded colleagues and Aspirational Wedding Planners to learn everything you need to know to firstly become and then grow as a talented, professional wedding planner who can make a positive impact on the wedding industry. It needs your talents and is waiting to welcome you!!

Kerry. xx

Kerry Jackson-Rider.

1 INTRODUCTION.

"Others see their possibilities in your reality" - (Unknown)

First of all you will probably want to know the answers to some questions such as:

What made me decide to become a Wedding Planner? How did I start out? Was it easy? What did I do first of all? What things did I find worked for me? What things didn't work so well? How did I decide to move forward? etc. so I will begin by answering those questions here and give you a little more background about the choices I made and am still making.

So, welcome to this book which is all about 'being' a Wedding Planner. I can totally understand why you want to become one as it's an industry and career which also attracted me and drew me in.

Back in 2009 I was struggling with where my career had ended up - as Head of Maths in a Pupil Referral Unit where I taught GCSE Maths to teenagers who really didn't want to be in class – in fact most of them really wanted to be anywhere else. That was challenging. Into this mix I threw planning for my own wedding and after a year of this I realised that with so many possibilities available through the internet etc. trying to pin down a venue let alone a whole bunch of suppliers was overwhelming and incredibly difficult to do whilst maintaining some reality with the budget that we had pre-set ourselves. We did manage to achieve an incredible wedding day in the end with help from lots of amazing people – who I continue to thank to this day, almost exactly four years later.

After this experience I felt strongly that I wanted to offer help and support to couples who find themselves in a similar position and one day I sat down to see if I could create a website. It turns out that I could – quite easily thanks to the wonders of Vistaprint – and so Your Day Your Way was born. I ordered some business cards and sat back wondering what I should do next.

I imagine some of you reading this have been there or maybe that's where you are at the moment – filled with a passion and desire to create something amazing which will not only help couples to have the wedding of their dreams but which also fulfills you and allows you to do something you love whilst making a living.

Don't get me wrong, I wasn't a total beginner having run my own businesses in the past and having had a succcessful career as a PR Consultant where I organised and promoted big events, corporate hospitality days etc. I was used to editing and publishing magazines and newsletters and, as a teacher, was highly organised but there were lots of new scary things to get to grips with like networking, social media, direct mail etc.

Well, read on to learn how I got from just sitting there in a bit of a daze, having just spontaneously created a new fledgling business, through many trials and errors to the place of relative comfort where I find myself today. It is due to the fact that I feel I have learned so much along the way that I know that If I share what I have learned it will save you and countless other Aspiring Wedding Planners a lot of time, money and soul-searching. When I was looking for answers early on, all I found was 'secrecy' like wedding planning was some secret cult open only to a few select (chosen by themselves of course!) members or I got fed a load of complete bull. So, I hope you will find this journey contains no bull and no fluff just clear, honest instruction on how you can start up and run your own successful Wedding Planning business.

Of course, I don't intend to just leave you hanging at the end of it either. I think some so-called 'mentors' don't even know the meaning of the word but I want to continue to give you the help that you will need to build up and grow your business and you can find out how in

Chapter 6 of this book.

If you decide to go it alone please do let me know how you get on so that we can all share in your success.

To your successful future as a wedding planner.

Kerry.

xx

www.kerryjacksonrider.co.uk

2 BEING A WEDDING PLANNER.

"The world really does need another [Wedding Planner], and we're waiting for YOU to bring it to us" - Marie Forleo.

So, first of all in this section I want you to spend a bit of time thinking about and answering the following important questions and jot down your thoughts before moving on:

1. What do YOU think a Wedding Planner does?

2. What makes a good Wedding Planner?

I will answer these and some other important questions and you should consider all these points before setting up in business as a Wedding Planner.

Answers:

1. What does a Wedding Planner do?

A wedding planner primarily helps and supports a couple on their wedding planning journey. This can be from start to finish or at any stage in between or by attending on the wedding day to oversee everything. We will talk more about the different services you can offer in Chapter 4. The help can take many forms but ideally you will be relieving them of the stress that comes with researching and securing venues for the ceremony and reception and hiring the myriad of suppliers who will bring their wedding vision to life. Negotiating contracts and liaison with them throughout will save the couple a lot of time and worry and you will have all the paperwork and contact details together in one place so they have complete peace of mind.

2. What makes a Good Wedding Planner?

You need to be organised with good people skills, creative and passionate. Personally I love beautiful flowers, good food/ wine and entertaining so this makes it very easy for me. Some planners love the fashion side so are big on bridal gowns and accessories. Others like the minute creative detailing which goes into setting up the reception venue. I think being psychic might also be helpful at times! and a preparedness for working unsocial and unconventional hours. So to sum up then, I think you need to have: personality and Style; creativity and good people/ management skills; excellent organisational and communication skills; a sense of humour, patience and flexibility.

3. Is it glamorous?

No! Not really unless you can call servicing the toilets, breaking down tables and running around in pain wearing high heels glamorous – thanks J-Lo!!

4. Is it fun?

Definitely Yes! and diverse. I love meeting lots of different people and I also get to make people's dreams come true.

5. How do you first have contact with a Bride and Groom to be?

Usually contact comes by email or by phone as an initial enquiry. If you have a contact form on your website then enquiries will come directly to your inbox from there. I always try to arrange a short (20 minutes) telephone conversation to get a feel for the wedding in terms of date, location, number of guests and budget as well as the bride's vision for the wedding and any specific details which may increase the complexity of the planning. You will need all this information and more to be able to ascertain what your fee may be.

6. Do you always arrange an Initial Consultation with the Bride and Groom to be?

Not always, it depends upon their location as they may be overseas or unable to meet up for a while due to circumstances. Often an extended telephone or Skype chat will allow you to gather more information as long as you are well prepared with the questions you need answers to in order to prepare a Quotation or Proposal as the next step.

7. What is a Quotation or Proposal?

This is one of the things that I found most

frustrating when I was starting as no-one was prepared to give away details of the elusive 'proposal'. I couldn't find a template anywhere, even on Google, it was a kind of holy grail. I now know that it is just a summary of the client's criteria for their wedding and how you intend to address their requirements with a price for doing so. There – it's not rocket science is it?!?

8. Should I have a Contract?

Yes definitely, a contract or terms and conditions should outline all the details of the agreement between yourself and the clients including the date and location of the wedding, their full names and contact details and, most importantly, it should set out very clearly both of your expectations for the partnership including hours and resources included in the fee, additional expenses for travel, accommodation etc. Be clear on whether you are attending and overseeing any pre- or post-wedding events including the rehearsal, rehearsal dinner, day before set up of the venue, clearing up on the evening, clearing up the next day, organising brunch or guest activities. This can lead to some confusion between the parties if the terms of the agreement are not clearly stated. The other important part is your payment and cancellation terms. I ask for a 50% deposit on signing of the contract with the balance 8 weeks before the wedding date. If you are adding on any known expenses take 50% of these up front also to cover your costs for holding deposits on hotel rooms, flights, train fares etc.

Wedding Project Management.

Planning a Wedding is Project Management pure and simple. You will have to project manage the whole thing, create a timetable of events, travel and accommodation. This will run from start to finish. If you are innovative and creative this will be helpful but most of all I think you need to be a great Problem Solver and that's how I like to think of myself. I like to solve BIG problems for people in the most efficient and cost-effective way for them. I also like to help and support them throughout their wedding planning journey and pride myself in doing this in a highly personal and professional way.

The key to effective problem solving is to have contingency plans and well negotiated contracts where every party knows exactly what the expectations are both of them and by them. You need to fully understand your role and the part you will play and demonstrate the attributes of a successful wedding planner. Don't forget your clients have probably hired you because:

a) they live in a different area from where the wedding is taking place
b) they require a destination wedding
c) they want to avoid long journeys
d) they don't have the local knowledge that you do
e) they are short of time
f) they wish to get the BEST value for their money
g) they want you to attend appointments with the best suppliers on their behalf
h) they want you to manage the venue and suppliers
I) they know YOU have unique ideas
j) they trust you to deliver on time and in budget

Key areas of Competence:

1.   **Planning and Organising** – you need to be meticulous about keeping everything on time and to the agreed budget. Detailed records should be kept and you must be aware of which stage all the activities are at. You are employed to save the clients time and remove the stress of planning and executing their wedding or event.

2.   **Introducing new Ideas** – you will be expected to bring new and exciting ideas to the table throughout the planning and design processes so it is vital that you keep up to date with developing and new trends in the wedding industry and changes in legislation etc. which might affect your client's wedding.

3.   **Be a Problem Solver** – the number of

venues and suppliers you will have to liaise with could be 30 or more and it is essential that you have good relationships with them, preferably you referred them having worked with them previously, have well negotiated contracts, contingency plans for wet weather etc. and that you know how to step in if anything goes wrong. Be sure to have up to date contact and mobile numbers as you will need this when you prepare your Running Order.

4.   **Sometimes you have to Compromise** – occasionally the budget you are working with will restrict what the clients can have so it is imperative to keep your Budget overview updated with supplier deposits and payments and to keep your couple in the loop and forewarned of any potential problems in advance. Sit down with them and make the necessary adjustments to keep on track and be sure to keep the venue and suppliers informed of any changes which need to be made.

5.   **It's not all Glamour** – there is, of course, a mundane side to planning a wedding which is the admin side but which is equally if not more important than the fancy bits. If invitations are not sent out on time and managed or if transportation is not booked it could be a disaster. I've also had to service the toilets at more than one wedding and high heels definitely do not stay on for long. **Top Tip**: Always bring flipflops and plasters!

6.   **Always Under Promise and Over Deliver** – I never promise to get my clients a discount from a venue or supplier but if I can then this is a nice surprise for them. Instead I always try to 'add value' by getting them little extras which will make a difference like room upgrades, champagne, spa treatments, a candlelight dinner etc.

Code of Ethics:

In the UK wedding planning is currently unregulated meaning that there is no specific body who is in charge of overseeing quality and performance. The closest thing we have to this is the UKAWP (The UK Alliance of Wedding Planners) who do a great job and have a Code of Ethics which you might like to look up and follow. I have adopted the following 'voluntary' code for myself:

- Respond to enquiries within 24 hours
- Respect client confidentiality
- Disclose any venues or suppliers you have a vested interest in
- Pass any discounts onto the client
- Never give client details to any third party unless for the sole purposes of the wedding
- Respect the copyright of all planners, co-ordinators, venues and suppliers
- Represent each client fairly and honestly

Abiding by this voluntary code of conduct will ensure that you and your business will operate with integrity, maintain and build a good reputation and result in recommendations and referrals from past clients, other planners, venues and suppliers.

Different Styles of Planners.

*Some Planners are more creative and like to specialise in décor and theme

*Others are more organisationally focused and enjoy the co-ordination and logistics

*Some are more traditional in their approach whilst others are contemporary even targetting the 'alternative'

*No matter what your personal preferences are there is room for everyone in this multi billion dollar market and, who says you have to stick with your original choice anyway? You need to make a decision in order to get started and then, as you learn more and develop your own style you will know which path is right for you.

Famous/ Celebrity Wedding Planners.

If you are not familiar with the work of the following people then I suggest you take some time to Google them, read all about them, take a look at some of their work and, when you decide who your favourites are, buy some of their books and even take any courses which they run and which you can afford to buy into:

Mindy Weiss, Martha Stewart, Marcy Blum, Sasha Souza, Preston Bailey, Colin Cowie, Randy Fenoli, David Tutera, Mark Niemierko, Sarah Haywood, Diann Valentine and Karen Bussen.

It is worth taking some time to really think about the sort of work you think you will be happy doing and for which clients. You can always revisit and modify later on.

3 THE PROCESS OF PLANNING A WEDDING.

"Dream Big. Start small. Act now." - Robin Sharma.

Let's Get Started!

So, we will look further at the Business of Being a Wedding Planner, how to start up and run your business, a little later on in Chapter 4 but let's get started on what's involved in the actual Process of Planning...

1. The Initial Consultation

Your initial enquiry from the client will probably come either by email, phone or via your website contact form, if you have one. The key information you need to know immediately is:

*When, where, number of guests, budget, type of ceremony and location. This will give you an indication of what you will likely be able to charge and is your way of pre-determining whether the client is an 'ideal' fit for you and your business. We will look more at this later on (p42).

If you decide from your first contact that you are suitably interested to take it further, the next step will be to arrange a meeting. I like to suggest a venue which I like and which may also be a possible fit for the couple's requirements OR I will go with their suggestion if it is important to them in terms of time, location etc. Your mission at this meeting is to LISTEN to everything the couple is telling you.

You can take along a portfolio of your work, or your Ipad or laptop if you would like to show them your most recent wedding – point out how much it cost to give them an idea and leave them with your business card.

*DON'T ask too many questions

You really only need to know the basics at this point as you are still weighing each other up

*DO tell them how you can help them and what makes you different

If they like you and you like them (ie. They are a good fit for you and you think they will happily pay your fee and value your work) you can arrange to send them an 'Outline & Quotation' (also called a Proposal) which will detail the work you are offering to do for them together with your fee for carrying out that work. Be sure to cover everything you can think of at this stage as you can always remove items if the couple don't want them included. Make sure your fee covers your expenses and the time and resources you expect to spend on the entire wedding.

Hoorah You Got the Wedding!

2. Congratulations! Now you need to send your **Contract or Terms & Conditions**, which should be drafted in the terms agreed to by the clients in your Proposal, and include your payment and cancellation terms, extras and expenses etc..

You will need to get a signed contract back from the clients together with a deposit BEFORE you start to do ANY work on their behalf. I take a 50% deposit as so much of the work is done straight away in terms of sourcing venues and suppliers, negotiating contracts etc. I ask for the balance to be paid 8 weeks prior to the wedding date. This covers the work required in the run up to the wedding including preparation of the Wedding Day schedule and management on the day.

## 3.	Choosing a Venue.

Top Tip: Always advise the couple to check that their date is available with the church or registrar before making a firm commitment to a venue.

Choosing a venue for the ceremony and reception is really important as it will dictate many of the other elements of the wedding. It will set the budget spend in terms of food and beverage (*see **Catering** below), entertainment, florals, hire in items etc. I normally recommend 3 -5 suitable venues based upon the couple's criteria and advise that visiting 2-3 is a good idea. Once the couple have chosen their favourite venue it is time to negotiate and sign the contract, paying a booking or holding fee to save the date.

Types of Venue.

There are many types of Venues available for weddings to suit ALL budgets and ranging from pubs and clubs, town or village halls, barns, marquees, boutique hotels, large resorts and football stadiums. The first step is to search for a suitable venue for the **Ceremony and Reception**. If it is a church wedding the couple may have a church in mind or they may need your help in choosing a Register office or venue. Use all your experience plus research as necessary and present them with 3 -5 suitable venues. Send them factsheets detailing location, spaces available with capacities, costs for food and drink options and accommodation. Most importantly CHECK that their date is available for their numbers and requirements.

Criteria for Choosing a Venue.

The criteria you will need to consider when sourcing and recommending Venues to your clients will include:
–   their Budget
–   number of Guests
–   chosen Date
–   chosen Location
–   will the ceremony and reception take place at the same Venue
–   are you also looking for a church or Register Office
–   are there any special dietary or other requirements which will affect the choice eg. Catering, cultural

Compile a list of 3-5 possible venues for the couple including the name, location, number of bedrooms, price of a three course meal with beverages, any entertainment or other restrictions (eg. Confetti, fireworks, candles). When the couple have chosen their favourites, normally 2-3, you will arrange to attend a site visit where the couple will be shown around the spaces and they can ask questions. If they like a venue you should request room rates, group booking discount, deposit and payment details and a draft contract.

Hotels and Resorts.

There are many different types of hotel – country and city, boutique, large and small. Many have a variety of spaces to suit all bugets and guest numbers. The benefit is in having accommodation on site which will reduce transportation costs and keep all the guests nice and handy. Larger or more expensive hotels will have a wide range of options for your clients to choose from and most will be included in the price which can represent a huge saving over a 'dry hire' venue.

Castles, Country Houses and Stately Homes.

Although a little more expensive, these venues provide a truly memorable opportunity if your clients' budget can stretch to it.

Catering.

I am including this section on Catering/ Food and Beverage here as it is such an important factor in choosing a venue which fits with the clients' budget.

Catering can be the biggest expense at a wedding

especially if guest numbers are high. Your clients' choice of menu and whether they opt for a sit down meal, buffet style or food stations, maybe a BBQ or hog roast or an Afternoon Tea. Budget and venue will be key in deciding the best way to cater. A tasting is important not only to taste the food and check the wines but also ask to see all the crockery, cutlery, glassware and serving options which are available to your client. Also tablecloths and napkins, candles, holders, table numbers and vases etc. that they are offering. If your clients dislike any of these items they can always hire in alternatives but this comes at a cost. There are some beautiful glasses, chargers and cutlery available for hire but the best will add to the bill for F&B and may need to be clawed back elsewhere on your Budget overview.

Make sure you know early on in the planning process of any special dietary requirements or allergies which any of the guests may have. Also, the expected number of child meals and vegetarian meals which will be required.

** I am also going to take the opportunity here to include a special overview and some case studies for you on **Marquee Weddings** just to alert you at this early stage to the fact that, although very popular - I have done many different Marquee weddings and I love them - but the couple don't always realise that they can be very expensive and fraught with potential difficulties therefore most wedding planners will charge <u>more than normal</u> to take this into account.

Marquee Weddings.

Marquee weddings are complex and are therefore one of the more expensive options due to the vast amount of suppliers and logistics involved. Everything has to be brought in and access can sometimes be a problem for generators and toilets which are mounted on trailers and cool units. Tables, chairs, all the catering equipment, bar, dancefloor etc. has to be brought in and set up AND broken down again after the event. The build will start several days before, depending upon the schedule of the contractors, and taken down several days after the wedding. Some people are lucky enough to own land in the family or have a big enough back garden to set up their own marquee whereas many country homes and estates offer a semi-permanent marquee structure which is sited within beautiful grounds. The Pavilion and Slaugham Place for example are mostly run by the caterers and these places provide a list of their recommended or preferred suppliers for you to choose from. There are also a lot of do's and don'ts with marquee weddings and details and contracts need to be checked really carefully to avoid pitfalls and disappointment later on. Some of the issues which come up are sound limiters which cut the power to the band or disco if the sound reaches or goes beyond a certain level. These are often used if there are residential buildings around the marquee. Access, as I mentioned, is often a problem especially if it is over a dirt track or grassy field and there is rain. Some of the trucks and trailers can have problems accessing the site. Where to locate portable toilets, generators and cool units can also be a problem and sometimes have to be sited further away than is really desirable. Clients often forget how much equipment is needed to produce a three course meal and drinks so are not prepared for the high cost of food and beverage which they encounter. This is also true for barns and village hall venues where virtually everything needed has to be hired in. Hire fees for some venues are really high and clients forget that the hire equipment, staffing and food and beverage is an additional cost. Be sure to discuss everything as early in the process as possible with clients who tell you they have already booked this type of 'dry hire' venue. I once had a young couple who came to me really excited as they had booked the barn of their dreams in the countryside. They said it was beautiful. I asked how much they had paid, or committed to, as they had thankfully only paid a deposit at this point. £6,000 they said. Their overall budget for the wedding was £12,000. I had to swiftly point out to them that I feared that just committing to this venue would eat up ALL of their budget and I arranged to speak with the recommended caterer immediately to get an idea of how much it was going to cost to furnish the building and supply food and drink to the guests. I was right of course and the couple had to cancel their booking and find an option which better suited the budget they had to work with. This turned out to be a very nice local hotel who were running a special 'all inclusive' offer which they managed to secure for just £5,000! With their venue, all the basics and a nice 3 course menu with welcome drinks, canapes, wine with the meal and champagne for the toast they had £7,000 left in their budget to spend on all their fancy bits. So, it turned out well in the end.

Another couple, who had booked a venue which did have its own tables and chairs but nothing else made a similar mistake as they were completely shocked when they discovered how much the recommended caterers would need to charge to cater for their 100 guests. As a result of the venue hire fee and the catering fee they were completely over-committed and had to cut back on areas of the wedding which had initially been in their priority list. This makes me sad and is why I feel I can only really help people fully if they come to me before they do anything else to discuss what they want for their wedding and a realistic budget. I can then advise them straight away based on their numbers, location etc. what is realistic and what isn't.

Having done many marquee weddings I do love them because you have a blank canvas which you can pretty much do with as you will. Brides have different creative ideas to incorporate which makes it personal and special for them but ultimately marquee weddings have a very traditional and elegant look and feel which I personally like. I also like the fact that everything can spill outside (weather permitting of course!) and there is nothing better on a sunny English summer afternoon and evening to stand back and watch everyone – children to grandparents – enjoying themselves with family and friends.

I love to put a string quartet under a canopy or sited in the ruins, as at Slaugham Place, and have waiter staff serving Pimms and champagne whilst the page boy is running amok and the groomsmen are eyeing up the ladies!

This leads us on to **Outdoor Weddings** in general. Some people get married in church and then have a marquee reception but others choose to also have their ceremony outdoors making use of a lovely garden or woodland area. Some firm favourites of mine include:

Beach Weddings
Woodland Weddings
Festival Weddings
Green/ Eco-friendly Weddings
Themed Weddings
Barns and Halls

and you will doubtless come across all these in your career, although sadly space permits me from going in to detail on all the endless possibilities and combinations here.

It is perfectly acceptable to add your own personal thoughts or experiences on each venue you recommend to the clients if you think it will be helpful to them in making their final choices.

Once the clients have chosen perhaps their favourite 2-3 venues that they would like to visit accompany them, if you can and if they want you to, to walk through the spaces and get as much information as you can. Be sure to get sample Menus, see the outside areas and bedrooms and get a feel for the team who will be co-ordinating with you on the wedding day.

Once the couple have chosen their venue you can contact them and negotiate a contract. When you are happy with this send it to the clients for signature and pay the deposit to the venue. Be sure to check the payment and cancellation details and make your clients aware of these and any other terms and conditions which may affect their use of the venue especially any restrictions regarding hiring in of suppliers, health and safety issues, set up and breakdown deadlines etc.

4. The Planning Meeting.

Next you can hold your very important Planning Meeting with the couple to go through ALL the details which will make their Wedding unique and personal for them. Allow around 2hrs for this face to face meeting which can take place at the venue you have just secured or another location. Go through everything in GREAT detail and make copious notes as this will form the basis of your planning and your running order for the Wedding day. Start with draft timings and an order of events which will evolve as you work through the planning stages.

Allow around two hours for this as you want to go through everything so that you can begin to build a picture of how the day will look. Create a Timeline for the wedding planning and give the couple a copy of this together with an initial Checklist to highlight for them what they should be doing at this time. I like to give these two items to the couple in stages, depending upon the lead in time to the wedding, otherwise they will get totally swamped and my job is to remove stress not increase it.

5. Budget Overview & Management.

A very important part of the Planning process is the Budget which you will have discussed and set with the client. It will be your job to create a spreadsheet to manage this in terms of both the estimated and actual costs. This is a living document which you will update possibly daily depending upon the size and complexity of the wedding. Start with what the couple want to spend on each element relative to their priorities and adjust it as quotes come in. This will allow you to keep things in proportion and report back to the couple if things are getting out of hand.

6. Supplier Search & Introductions.

Researching and sourcing suppliers is one of the most time consuming parts of the wedding planning process. When you know what Suppliers your clients wish to hire for their wedding and their priorities and vision you will be able to make recommendations based on your experience and careful research as needed. Recommend no more than 3 – 5 suppliers in each category who you think will fit the bill and send factsheets to the clients with details, pricing structures and any additional information you think may be helpful. Again, be sure to CHECK their availability BEFORE putting them forward for the wedding.

I prefer to recommend up to 3 in each category in line with the couple's criteria and let them choose which suppliers they would like to meet with and see examples of their work. When they have chosen their favourites it is time to negotiate and sign contracts when a booking or holding deposit will be payable to save the date.

Categories of Suppliers.

Catering/ food and beverages (if not included with the venue), florist, cake maker, photographer, videographer, entertainment, hire items, production, lighting, hair and make up, bridal party attire, décor items – the list is endless but these are the main ones.

Tastings.

Menu tastings for the couple will be arranged by the venue or with the caterers if external suppliers when the wines and champagne and any specially prepared cocktails should also be sampled and the opportunity taken to look at the venue or caterer's linens, glassware, cutlery and tableware including serving platters, uniforms etc. in case they are not to the clients' liking. You must point out to them that an additional fee will be incurred for hiring in alternatives, which they may not immediately be aware of.

Etiquette, Culture and Traditions.

Always be ready to advise any members of the bridal party regarding etiquette and traditions in terms of seating plans, receiving line, speeches, order of service etc. and be mindful of any traditions, specific religious and dietary requirements which may affect all or some of the bridal party and their guests. If in doubt ask and do as much research as is necessary to get it right. You may need to bring in experts in some cases which, again, may not be immediately obvious to the clients.

When the couple have chosen 2-3 photographers,

florists etc. that they would like to meet with, arrange the meetings and accompany your clients so that you can make the introductions. Make sure you have fully briefed the suppliers beforehand about the couple, their budget, their requirements and their overall vision for the wedding.

Top Tip: Remember that EVERY supplier you put forward represents you and your brand/ ethos.

Usually, the couple will bond immediately with at least one of the suppliers you have recommended in each category and ask you to move forward with negotiating a contract. Again, be sure to check the terms and conditions carefully, referring the clients to any possible red lights. Once they are happy they should sign and pay a deposit to secure their date. Enter the cost, payment and date AND the date the balance payment is due on the Budget overview.

When you have all the basics in place ie. The venues, church or registrar and suppliers are booked it is time to sit down once again with your clients to hold a **Design Meeting** where you can thrash out all the finishing touches that will be required to make the couple's wedding truly unique and in keeping with their wedding vision. Again, I recommend allowing around 2 hours for this and if you can get the couple to clear this space in their diaries and try not to take phone calls etc. you will get the best result for all concerned.

7. Design Concept.

Many couples will come to you with a clear idea of how they want their Wedding to look but some others may look to you for help with the entire Design concept. It is up to you to learn the basics so that you can help and advise them on this aspect of the planning, if you include it in your services of course. If it is an area which really resonates with you I would suggest adding it as a bespoke Consultancy service as it may set you apart from the competition and shows that you offer something 'extra'.

I am going to give you quite a lot of information on **'The Art of Wedding Design'** in Chapter 5 and I recommend that, if this aspect really interests you, that you do some more research and take a course or two to really cement your understanding and so that you can help your clients as much as possible.

8. Payment of Venue and Suppliers.

Continue to liaise with the venues and suppliers throughout and manage the payment schedule with a spreadsheet so that you know exactly which payments are due and when. Make sure you check and double check all the paperwork you receive as mistakes can and do happen. Times of arrival, set up, start and finish for bands for example are crucial to the smooth running of the evening. Transportation is another area of concern. If you are booking limousines or double decker buses make sure you and the company agree the timings, routes, access etc. and have back up contact numbers just in case.

9. The Running Order.

All the work you have been doing over the past, let's say 12 months, comes to fruition with creation of the Running Order or Wedding Day schedule. This is where all the important details are stored – contact names, numbers, back ups, timings, who does what, when, where and how. Accuracy and agreement of the content of this document are vital to ensure smooth running of the day although, trust me, someone will do their best to screw it up for you on the day! It happens every time but with this schedule in place you will find it much easier to move to Plan B without everyone knowing!

You will begin work on the Running Order around two weeks before the Wedding, when everything is confirmed and in place. This Wedding Day Schedule will contain all the contact details, timings and who will do what, when and where covering the days running up to the Wedding day and also the day after – depending upon the duration of the wedding, set up times and pre-/ post- wedding events. The accuracy of this schedule and <u>compliance by all parties</u> is essential for the smooth running of the wedding day.

You will need to contact the Ceremony and Reception venues and ALL suppliers to double check contact names and mobile numbers for the day PLUS get back ups in the event of unforeseen circumstances. Ensure that everyone involved shares the same understanding of what time they will arrive to set up and breakdown, deliver the bridal flowers etc. and get confirmations by email before you finalise the Running Order. If there is a dress code include this together with delivery and collection protocols, floor plans and details of the Bridal party.

**Send a final copy to EVERYONE 2 days before the Wedding and obtain confirmation of receipt.

10. Pre-Wedding events.

It is unlikely that you will be asked to get involved with organising the hen and stag do's but the ceremony rehearsal, either at the church or at the venue, followed by a relaxing, informal rehearsal dinner for the bridal party is a nice way to meet everyone and lead in to the big day.

11. The Wedding Day has Arrived!

With your Running Order in hand (or on a clipboard!) you are now ready to put on a show and bring this baby home! You will be on site for at least 12 hours today to manage and oversee the set up of the Ceremony and Reception spaces through the Ceremony and Reception until the last guest and supplier has left the building so make sure you're wearing comfy shoes and don't expect to eat or drink until late evening.

Top Tip: Seriously pack some snack bars, water and any medications just in case plus Polos – I always get asked for mints and deodrant!

You will make sure the ceremony and venue are set up to the Bride's satisfaction and oversee that the suppliers know where to go and what to do.

You will be required to:

*Oversee the start of the Ceremony

*Oversee the Catering set up and serving

* Oversee the Entertainment arrival and set up

* Oversee the Bar set up and make sure it remains well stocked and staffed, glasses are collected promptly

* Check the toilets regularly to make sure they are re-stocked and clean at all times, ensure candles are replaced and lit promptly

*Oversee the Evening catering

*Oversee the departure of the Bride & Groom and all the guests

*Oversee the breakdown of the event and the departure of the suppliers

This is a good place to include information about what you should have in your '**Emergency Kit**' which will accompany you to every wedding. I also like to make sure that I or the venue have access to a good supply of umbrellas, parasols, wellies, flipflops, shawls depending on the anticipated weather.

Emergency Kit.

While we always hope we don't have any emergencies on the Wedding Day, it's always better to be safe than sorry. Here's a list (not exhaustive by any means! - just use your common sense regarding location ie. Water, beach – mosquitos, sand flies etc.). The Maid of Honour can look after a bag of the Bride's personal items including lipstick, perfume etc. if your hair and make up artist isn't staying close by. My own 'box' of goodies, in suitably random order, contains the following:

*Paracetemol (other pain reliever of choice), Rennie, Migraleve

*Plasters, antiseptic wipes and cream, tissues

*Bottle of water, breath mints/Polos!), snack/cereal bars

*Talc/ Chalk (to cover up any make up/ stains on Bride's dress)

*Clear nail varnish, nail file

*Dressmaker's pins/ safety pins, mini sewing kit

*Dental floss, eye drops, baby wipes

*Deodorant (men's and women's) and perfume

*Extra earring backs

*Tights – natural

*Black men's socks, men's hair gel

*Hairgrips/ hairbands, hairspray, small mirror, basic make up for touch ups - concealer, lipstick, mascara

*Antibac hand gel and wipes, sunscreen, mosi repellent, bite spray/ cream

*Matches, torch, Sellotape, double-sided tape, extension cord, Blue Tack

*Small scissors, tweezers

*Drinking straws (so Bride doesn't smudge her lippy!)

*Tampons/ sanitary towels/ pant liners

*Brush/ comb

*Cash, business cards, your Mobile phone with EVERYONE's number (duplicated from Running Order) and BACK UP numbers. **Top Tip**: Make sure your phone is FULLY charged and keep your charger handy.

12. Post-Wedding events.

A brunch attended by all the wedding guests who have stayed over is a nice way to round off the wedding experience for everyone. Often clients will arrange a farewell BBQ if the weather is good enough or some activity that their guests can enjoy before departing.

Troubleshooting.

A huge part of being a Wedding Planner is managing your clients' expectations and those of their guests. Never promise something you can't deliver in fact ALWAYS under-promise and over-deliver. Manage and control the amount of choices you give your clients eg. 2-3 recommendations for suppliers is plenty and 3-5 venue recommendations. Never let them make appointments with more than 2-3 of each. Always have a Plan B and a 'wet weather' plan. Remember: It's all in the details!

Happy Planning!

Next up...... We'll take a look at **'The Business of Being a Wedding Planner'.**

4 THE BUSINESS OF BEING A WEDDING PLANNER.

"The best advice I could give anyone is to spend your time working on whatever you are passionate about in life." - Sir Richard Branson.

There are a few things you really need to get clear on <u>before</u> you start up your wedding planning business which is why we're going to set about answering these important questions as your very first 'Assignment'!

1. **What's your WHY?** Why are you setting up as a Wedding Planner, who do you want to serve, what do you want to achieve?

2. **What will be your business name, brand**

and logo design? What colour/s will you choose and why? (be sure to check for the symbolism and cultural/ religious meanings and traditions associated with different colours AND their effects on people's moods). Do you want to use a monogram made of your initials perhaps or a picture or image which reflects your business style?

3.   **Who is your ideal client**/ target audience ie. Which segment of the public/ market do you want to serve? You will need to know <u>who</u> it is that you want to work with so that you can market and sell your products and services to them.

4.**What are the basic things YOU will need to get started?** You will need a website, with the facility to add a blog, and some business cards.

5. **How will you get some clients?** How will you find your first work? This will depend upon your chosen target market and where they are to be found eg. Facebook, Twitter etc. We will look at Marketing and Social Media Marketing later on in this chapter...

Go out and do some networking – maybe join a group such as BNI or a business women's group, go and introduce yourself to venues and suppliers to establish good relationships which you can build on and call upon in the future as your business builds.

Get yourself in front of brides and grooms – so sign

up and attend a few local wedding fairs and see which ones work for you and your chosen market.

6. Which Services will you offer and How will you Price your Services?

Wedding Planning IS a business after all and one of the first things you will need to consider is HOW you want to spend your time and HOW you are going to make money out of it.

**Remember: Your Time = Money.

You will need to decide at the outset whether you are going to set a minimum budget requirement, how many weddings you want to plan each year and how much you are going to charge per wedding. Let's say you want to do 6/8 weddings per year. If you set a minimum budget of £50,000 with a minimum fee of £5,000 you would hope to bring in £30,000 – 40,000 minimum per year.

Remember this is a gross figure before you take off all your expenses and a salary for yourself and is a pretty healthy amount. Compare this to doing the same number of weddings at say £2,000 which would only bring you in £12,000 – £16,000 and you can see that you would probably want to increase if not double the amount of weddings you do to bring in £24,000 – £32,000. You will have to ask yourself do I want to and can I physically service this number of clients by myself? **If you decide to come on board with me for private Mentoring sessions I will help you to create your Services Menu and set your Pricing etc. (see Chapter 6 for more details on 'What YOU Can Do Next')

The Range of Wedding Planning Services.

Many wedding planners offer all of the services below and some offer only one or two. It really depends on how you like to work with the couple. I like to be fully involved from start to finish which is why I only offer a Full wedding planning service. I have found that the other options don't really work for me but you must see what works best for you.

* **Full Wedding Planning**

* **Partial Wedding Planning**

* **On the Day Management**

* **Bespoke Consultancy Services**

You can offer all the elements of the wedding planning process as stand alone items if you wish eg. Venue sourcing, Supplier sourcing, Budget management, creating a Wedding Day schedule, set up and décor. The prices of all these services range widely across the country and from planner to planner. Some people prefer to do what they enjoy the most or are best at.

Your Pricing.

Deciding what to charge as a wedding planner is another complex issue. If you check websites around the country you will see that the price varies widely from region to region and for different services. People always say "charge what you're worth" which is an unknown quantity in itself and it is especially hard for new wedding planners to find the place where they are comfortable pitching their services and price. I think that's the key though, that you are comfortable with what you're asking for. If you feel it's not working for you or you get a lot of comments that you're too cheap or too expensive then you can always re-evaluate and tweak your pricing structure.

As a guideline most of the planners in the UK charge a percentage fee of the couple's overall wedding budget of 10-15%. So, if your couple have a budget of £30,000 you would charge them £3000 - £4500 depending upon the criteria of the wedding and which fee you are most comfortable with. Location and guest numbers will also play a part as a wedding with 40 guests with that budget will, in theory, be much easier to co-ordinate than one with say 100 guests. I will say that I have mostly found in the past that you usually end up doing more work than you expected on every wedding, for whatever reason, so my best advice to you would be to **never price yourself lower than you are**

comfortable with as you will surely live to regret it. Although it is possible to ask for more money, and you should have an 'extras' clause in your contract to cover such eventualities, this can be an uncomfortable process and is not at all desirable.

The style of planning you want to do will create the Services you will offer to your clients. For instance, I decided in 2011 that I wanted to operate a 'one stop shop' style approach whereby I WANT to handle everything on my clients' behalf. I enjoy arranging travel and accommodation, logistics and transportation. I am also quite traditional in my approach opting for Elegance and Style over 'quirky' trends and enjoy the Design process.

The pricing of Wedding Planner services is an area which is often debated but really comes down to your personal preferences and the Services you choose to offer.

As I said, most planners in the UK will charge a set fee based on a % of the overall budget spend which is usually 10 -15% eg. If your couple has a budget of £30,000 your fee would be £3000 - £4500 based on the location, guest numbers, complexity etc. of the wedding.

Other methods are to just charge a straight set fee eg. £1200 for On the Day management – it has to be a price which YOU have calculated to cover your costs and make you a profit and needs to be based on the amount of time you will spend working for the client.

There are, of coure, pros and cons to both ways of charging and you will come across clients who feel you are charging too much or who want a breakdown of the costs so that they can try to work out how much you charge 'per hour'. It is up to you whether you want to get in to this kind of detail – I can guarantee you will at first! - but my advice would be to avoid discussing your time specifically and to make it about the service you are providing and the value and benefits which you are offering to the clients.

**I do know planners who work solely on commission but this is abroad and receiving 'commissions' is not a widely accepted method of covering your fee in the UK.

Your Business Name, Branding & Logo.

The next important thing to think about is your business name, branding and logo which you will use on all your on and offline marketing materials including your website, business cards, social media profiles, your blog, newsletter etc. You will want to choose colours and a name which reflects your chosen niche in the market. Try to use a unique name – maybe your own name or a variation on it – eg. My business name is Kerry Jackson-Rider and the company name Tania Tapel is very cleverly created from its founder's name Anita Patel. Also try to reflect your USP (unique selling proposition) ie. What makes **YOU** and your business unique in all your materials and messaging that you put out from the start. If your budget allows it a good way to get started is to use a web/ design company who will not only design and create your website (which may include a blog) for you but also come up with brand ideas, logos and print materials for you.

How Do I Get My First Work?

One of the best ways to gain experience as a new wedding planner is to offer to plan weddings and events for friends, family and colleagues. This will give you the opportunity to start to build up a portfolio of images of your work – be sure to take photos of everything you do (I am terrible at this!) and you can add these to your website gallery with Testimonials from your satisfied and happy clients. Another way into the industry is through a 'work experience' placement which, as most of you will know, is quite hard to come by. Be confident – approach venues and suppliers to start to build relationships, be visible on social media platforms, attend local wedding fairs to meet brides, network like mad and set up a photoshoot to showcase your talents.

Promoting Your New Business.

As soon as you have your shiny new business cards to hand you can start to network with venues and suppliers to introduce yourself and start to build up relationships. You can ask a venue you like if you could arrange a photoshoot there – offer them some free photos which they can use in exchange – and choose some suppliers to help you set the scene, most importantly, a good photographer to capture all your hard work. *Check first that they are happy to let the venue have free photos before you negotiate this. Be sure to credit everyone involved when you publish the photos to your website, blog and social media. Add them to your gallery and the Ipad or laptop portfolio which you are building to show clients.

PR, Advertising, Marketing, Social Media etc.

PR (public relations) is free, usually editorial, publicity about you and your business which you should share everywhere you can. Get to know the bridal magazines, both on and offline, which serve your target market, seek out the relevant Bloggers and online magazines.

Advertising is paid for, most often display, and

usually expensive.

Marketing is everything else including **Social Media Marketing**, your website, blog, leaflets, branded merchandise etc.

Marketing.

Your Website is your biggest marketing tool which is why your name, logo design and branding is so important. I chose the template for my Wedding Planning Workshop slide presentations because my corporate colour is 'Ruby Red' – if you've attended any of my workshops did you actually make that connection?!? I do tend to choose Red for my profile pictures, text on Twitter etc. In order to keep the branding going and even for the cover of this book as my profile picture with the red is easily recognisable.

Top Tip: Marketing basically includes everything you say about your business, everywhere you are seen. This is why it's **SO** important to be clear on your target audience and your brand message.

Social Media Marketing.

With so many platforms ie. Facebook, Twitter, Linked In, Tumblr etc. it is important to find the ones that work best for you and are where your audience is. It can take up a lot of your time so you will need to prioritise. I would say that #ww Wedding Wednesday and #ff Follow Friday on Twitter are useful and Facebook gives you more space to promote yourself and your ideas with photos.

5 THE ART OF WEDDING DESIGN.

"The world is full of sources of inspiration; the key is really looking, listening and taking in what is in front of you and around you" - Preston Bailey.

There are a vast number of Design styles out there and each can be adapted to suit the space that you are working with. All spaces are different – even marquees have different shapes and layouts – many hotels and ballrooms will have fixtures and fittings which you will either need to work with or cover up. This goes for carpets, walls, paintings, stages etc. and you should always check what you can and can't do under the terms of the contract with the venue BEFORE making any promises to the couple as to what you can achieve on their behalf. Also, unless they have a very good budget production and equipment hire like this is very costly and compromises like drapes, chair covers etc. may be needed.

The **Styles** that we are probably most familiar with in the Wedding world include rustic/ country, Shabby Chic, Minimalist, Asian and Vintage/ Retro. We will usually look to work with symmetry and try to create a feeling of harmony in our placement of tables etc. Again, the resources you have to work with will to some extent dictate the outcome you are able to achieve but colour and shape will play a big part in your designs and for most brides their table centrepieces will be an important area to focus on. These are often used to create **the WOW! factor** as is the cake so it is important that these are sited strategically for emphasis and impact.

I tend to use **Naturalism** a lot, which uses inspiration from nature and works especially well with a 'green' or eco-minded bride, because I like to incorporate any natural elements within the venue or outside ie. Stone, wood, brick, sand, foliage, water etc. This would also use cotton and linen, bamboo, shells, natural colours from the earth tones palette (browns, greens, beige, white etc.) This also works very well with rustic and country styles where use of big wooden tables, wooden platters, twigs, lemons, olive branches etc. - you see I have moved into the realms of a Tuscan/ Italian-style rustic wedding like I did at Jamie

Oliver's Threadneedles restaurant!) This works well in an outdoor or barn setting where you have the natural elements of stone and wood and trees.

Geometric and modern designs work well with a **Minimalist** style and these are often created with a lot of white and a strong accent colour, often black, maybe orange, aqua or bright pink. This can look stunning in the right setting so a modern, rectangular shaped room with a nice light wooden floor and pale painted walls and maybe lots of glass to let in natural light

Due to the fascination of many brides with **Vintage/ Retro** styles we tend to see a rather eclectic mixture of items and ideas incorporated into wedding themes. This can be done very stylishly indeed and creates a fun atmosphere – perfect for an outdoor, **Summer wedding** with perhaps a **'Vintage Afternoon Tea'** or **'Garden Fete'** theme with the use of bunting, hay bales, fairground stalls, jam jars of flowers etc.

Principles of Design include Emphasis – ie. What the eye is drawn to so this could be the table centrepieces, the cake or another focal point; Balance – usually found through symmetrical placing of tables etc.; Harmony when the mixing and matching of styles and elements looks and feels right and Repetition – through use of shapes and sizes eg. Your tables, use of colour. Proportion and Scale are also important to bear in mind as these will affect the overall look and feel of the finished space and help with your successful achievement of a balanced and harmonious setting.

We would more often than not achieve these things organically as we are working to decorate our spaces, a lot of which is trial and error and doesn't always match our designs for various reasons but, as I said before, if this is an area which you want to get really proficient at read, research and study the best in the business.

Use of Colour Palettes.

We all have our own ideas of which colours go together and which clash and this can be a very personal thing. If your bride tells you she wants to work with a palette which makes you go eek! Start by asking to see her cuttings, **Pinterest** boards etc. so that you can double check that she actually means the colours which have leapt into your mind. If you are still unsure show her how you can add in another colour to soften it or maybe a metallic to lift it or take her to your florist or decorator and get them to put some items in the colours together and see what she says. If she still loves it you will have to go with it!

My favourite colours for weddings are soft pinks, blushes, creams and white with a metallic element, I love gold, but silver, copper and bronze work well. I think this gives the most elegant and romantic look. Of course, different colours are associated with different moods, symbolism and evoke different feelings in different people. I won't get into the Primary, Secondary, Tertiary colour thing here but here are a few tips on choosing colours which may come in handy with your couples:

Red, Orange and Yellow – are the warm colours. Red is symbolic of Passion and Love eg. Red roses and Valentine's Day but also of strength and anger. Orange and Yellow remind us of Summer and the sun and are generally conducive to feelings of 'happiness'.

Blue, Purple and Green – are the cool colours and are symbolic of calmness and the sea. They can also produce feelings of 'sadness' in some people. Blue is the most popular colour. Green is the colour of balance and harmony. Violet is a very gentle, soothing colour and is often included in a Wedding colour palette in varying shades.

White is the colour of purity, minimalism and simplicity whereas Black is often associated with funerals and negative feelings. As we know, the combination of Black and White is stunning and impactful and is very often used in Wedding décor.

Brown is the colour of earth and nature and all its tones are soothing. Chocolate brown used with shades of orange makes a lovely basis for a Wedding palette especially for an Autumn wedding.

There are also cultural responses and symbolism associated with certain colours – green is the sacred colour of Islam and is considered 'lucky' in Ireland. In England it is considered 'unlucky'. Purple is associated with royalty. Red, as I said, is associated both with love and anger.

Colour also affects our behaviour so always know what mood you are trying to create in each of your spaces and vary it as necessary. You can keep a colour theme running throughout but make sure that the finished product is suitable for the environment for instance you probably wouldn't want to use the same florals for your church focal point as you would in your nightclub setting...

Finishing Touches.

How do you make your Designs unique and personal to your clients? Well, you will have listened well and got to know them both in your initial consultation, found out their priorities for the wedding in your Planning meeting and really dug down into their wedding vision in your Design meeting. So by the time you come to work on your Design Concepts you should have a really good understanding of what they love and hate, what they would like to achieve, budget permitting, and any areas where they really want you to pull out all the stops. If at this point there is anything you feel you need more clarity on don't be afraid to ASK or set up an extra brief meeting to answer any outstanding questions you may have. Use everything you know about them to finalise your concepts for each space which you are using. You may have a church and a reception venue or a hotel where the room is being used for the ceremony and then re-set for the reception and even re-set again for the party/ dancing. The spaces you are working with and the budget you have will dictate pretty much how you will work. It is down to you to work out how you can achieve the best possible outcome in line with the couples' vision.

So, you have your Style – Vintage, Minimalist, Classic, Rustic etc.; your Principles – naturalism, minimalism, eclectic; and your Colour Palette. You will know the Mood you are trying to create and your Budget. So, what can you do now?

You will need to consider the floor, the walls, the windows, the ceiling, the doorways and any fixed features like a stage, bar, plinths, fireplace etc. You will need your floor layout and your table plan to hand. You will have asked the venue manager or co-ordinator for their suggestions for laying out tables and chairs with your number of guests, also check on serving stations, access for the waiting staff and where you will site your singer or live entertainment.

It can be really hard if you are dealing with a carpet which the bride hates but can't afford to cover. Sometimes you just have to work with it in terms of colour and remind her that when all the tables, chairs and guests are in place there will usually be very little of that carpet left on show. Wall colour again can be an issue and, if money allows, you can arrange to line the walls with drapes (if permitted by the venue – not all will allow this). Curtains which don't match and the colours of banquet chairs can also be a problem. If your bride hates all these things you have to ask what she actually liked about the venue to make her book it in the first place and if it is because it was the only thing they could afford within their budget then she really is going to have to work with it not against it. This may mean adjusting her preferred colour palette to incorporate the colours in the room. Once again, this is why I prefer to work with my clients right from the very start so that some of these issues can be avoided.

If money is no object then every problem can be sorted and you can just steam ahead. You may be hiring in different tables, chairs, linens, glassware, crockery and cutlery. You have your colours sorted and the florist knows exactly what the bride wants for her centrepieces etc. Try to keep the table as uncluttered as possible as people forget that wine and water bottles, salt and pepper, butter dishes, bread baskets etc. can take up a lot of space. I always like candles on the table, either tall (if allowed by the venue) or votives in pretty holders which match your theme. I personally prefer nice Chiavari or other banquet chairs to chair covers but sometimes it is the best way to cover up standard banquet or conference chairs and with coloured sashes looks very professional and orderly.

Here is an Article I wrote which contains a lot of interesting Design details:

'Back to Nature' - Inspiration for a Woodland Themed Wedding.

I always try to incorporate nature and the surroundings into my designs as much as possible, especially for Destination Weddings, when I will use sand, shells, wood, natural stone, brick or whatever's available. I'm also especially fond of incorporating trees into outdoor wedding settings where they can make wonderful natural canopies to shade from the sun or you can attach fabrics to create gorgeous sweeping canopies. Lanterns and lights hanging through the trees also bring a magical feel as the day turns into evening.

Always try to let the outside flow in and vice versa with a gentle transition between spaces especially if the indoor space is cavernous or a bit dark. If you are hiring a marquee topiary works well just outside the door, maybe forming a walkway,

and small trees and planters dotted around inside can enhance your layout. Naturalistic design can incorporate inspirations from anything in nature. Natural colours from the earth tones palette eg. browns,
tans, greens, white and off-white can be set off with bold colourful accents or use of metallics. Use of twigs – either sprayed to achieve a certain colour or natural – can be used in your table centrepieces or in floor standing arrangements. You can wire lemons or wicker hearts onto these, dcponding upon your theme, and they work really well with any type of Rustic styling. Outdoor ceremony settings using haybales or tree trunks or chairs carved from wood and wooden arches will work well within this theme.

The use of any natural water eg. a fountain, lake, moat or pond and ruined walls or buildings create interest. Natural brickwork and stone, exposed timber, cobbled paving etc. can all be emphasised although I wouldn't advocate having all your finishes in the same material, break it up or add something ie. a wooden floor and a natural brick wall/ backdrop will need some foliage, colourful floral accents, tall candelabra and subtle lighting. How about using different textures for fabrics including cottons, linen, jute, raffia etc. and go strong with your napkins, table runners or chairbacks. Can you feel how cosy and welcoming that space would be? Then you can go on to add in your tables, chairs and finishing touches...

---oOo---

Top Tip: If you haven't already been given design boards or an overall theme by the Bride this is the time to get down to the nilly gritty. Introduce her to Pinterest, in the unlikely event that she doesn't already have a range of boards for her special day!, and have your Ipad or laptop ready to show her designs and elements which match her criteria. If she doesn't yet have a theme in mind she will doubtless have a colour palette with which you can work and an idea of the style or overall look she wants to create. Work together on this and then you can produce either a Pinterest board or concept board in the following days for her approval. This is also a good time to give the couple an up to date Timeline and Checklist for their next jobs.

6 WHAT CAN <u>YOU</u> DO NEXT?

"There is no passion to be found playing small in settling for a life that is less than you are capable of living" - Nelson Mandela.

So, there you have it. We have looked at what's involved in Being a Wedding Planner, The Process of Wedding Planning, The Business of Being a Wedding Planner and The Art of Wedding Design. If you go ahead and work through this book, answering all the questions I've asked you to consider and taking notice of my tips and suggestions, you will have everything you need to get started on setting up and running your new wedding planning business.

As I said at the beginning, it is not my intention to simply abandon you at this stage with all this new information and a sense of overwhelm so, "Congratulations" if you know you want to **be the best** and are ready to **invest in yourself** and move forward with your ideas by signing up to take advantage of **private Mentoring sessions** with me. I will look forward to hearing all about your business plans & objectives and to helping you get started in your new career. If you would like to come onboard with one of my 'exclusive' Training & Mentoring programmes you can **Call to speak to me on +44 (0)7860 580794** and email me at hello@kerryjacksonrider.co.uk and see more details of the training available on the website at www.kerryjackson-rider.co.uk/wedding-services/wedding-planner-training-mentoring-worldwide

So, what else can YOU do now in order to learn more and move yourself forward to the next level?

- private Mentoring with Kerry

- VIP Day

- 6 Month Intensive Training & Mentoring programmes

- the ULTIMATE Wedding Planner Training & Mentoring programme

- Luxury/ Destination Wedding Planner Training intensive in TOP wedding locations in Italy

What will I learn through completing an 'exclusive' Training & Mentoring programme with Kerry?

We will take an in-depth look at all of the <u>key areas</u> of Wedding Planning building up your skills and knowledge as we go and including:

* Creating these very important documents - the Proposal & Quotation, Activity Report and Wedding Day Schedules

* Budget and Timeline management and overviews

* Types of Ceremony – helping your clients with the legal requirements, etiquette, vows and speeches

* Working with different Venues – you will have the chance to visit TOP wedding venues and make useful and lasting contacts

* Working with Suppliers – you will have the chance to meet with the best suppliers who are experts in their field and be able to work with them

* Décor and Theme – we will get creative! and work through design concepts, creating layouts and Pinterest boards

* How to run a successful Wedding Planning

business

* Advanced Management and Scheduling techniques

* PR and Marketing

* Growing your Business

A Special Offer Just for YOU!

Once again, I would like to take this last opportunity to encourage you to **SIGN UP for private Mentoring with me** as it is SO important to keep up the momentum that we have created for you here – I don't want YOU to feel that you have just been left on your own to 'get on with it' - my aim is to do the best I can for my students.

So, to help YOU learn even more and get your new Wedding Planning business up and running even faster as **a Special Offer for you and as a thank you** for buying and reading this book "Start Up and Run Your Own Successful Wedding Planning Business" I am offering you **a Half Price VIP Day** when you Quote: Book1/11/15 (*offer valid until 31/07/16).

Call +44 (0)7860 580794 NOW to book your 'exclusive' VIP Day as places are limited and subject to availability.

7 ARTICLES, PRESS & BLOGS.

Here are a few press cuttings, articles and blog posts I have written to show you that "if I can do it" so can you!!

My 4 Top Tips for Choosing the Perfect Photographer for YOU.

When it comes to choosing a professional to carry out any element of your Wedding it can be hard to define exactly what it is that YOU are hoping to achieve and also to know the right things to check before you make a commitment. I hope these 4 Top Tips will help you to feel more confident when approaching a photographer and help you go to them with a clear idea of how you want them to help you.

Photocredit: Peter Lane Photography

1. Do you like their Style?

Check online portfolios, blogs and social media to see a wide body of work. Does it fit with your vision of how you want your wedding photos to look?

2. Do they offer everything you need?

Do they produce only digital images or albums as well? Do they offer an online gallery where your friends and family can view and order photos? Will there be one or two photographers attending on your Wedding day to capture all the action?

3. Will they do a pre-Wedding shoot?

Eg. a 'get to know you' session or engagement shoot for you and WHERE will this take place? Is this included in the price quoted or is it an extra? Be sure to check whether any travel expenses or accommodation costs will be incurred and get a price for these.

4. Be sure you're getting what YOU want for the price stated

Check their T&C's thoroughly for deposit and final

payment details, copyright, licensing etc. Check that the hours of attendance cover your start and finish times. If you want them to start early to cover bridal preparations or stay late to capture a firework display or you both leaving there may be an extra charge for this. If in doubt ASK all these questions when you have your first telephone or face to face meeting to avoid any disappointment later on.

---oOo---

A 'Game of Thrones' Themed Wedding Inspiration

With Season 4 of this epic fantasy series due out at the beginning of April I was asked to write an article on "**How to Have a Game of Thrones themed Wedding**'. This is the design board I made to help me focus and you can read the article itself here: http://t.co/auFZfDLHzZ
Watch the new trailer
here: http://t.co/0Tz29ih7V2 it's awesome! I cannot wait to see King Joffrey's wedding in all it's spectacular glory…

'Game of Thrones' is a great choice if you are looking for a 'themed' wedding as there is so much you can incorporate. See my full 'Game of Thrones' Pinterest board here:

www.pinterest.com/LuxuryWedding/a-game-of-thrones-themed-wedding/

How Can YOU Enjoy the Wedding of Your Dreams Without Breaking the Bank?

This is such an age old question but so completely relevant in today's tough economic climate. It's simple! Budget, Budget, Budget AND by taking the advice of professionals whose mission in life is to help YOU have the Wedding you've always dreamed about at a price you can afford! I don't mean that you need to rush out and pay someone for service straight away but sage advice is often givon freely and willingly by venues and suppliers who are always keen to help. We all know that money is a lot harder to come by and a lot harder to keep hold of than it once was and Brides and Grooms to be everywhere are rightly looking to get the very best value from their pound or dollar. It makes sense to spend some time on your pre-research to try and tie everything in as neatly as possible before you go ahead and start to make firm bookings. Of course a Wedding Planner is the ideal person to help you with this and save your valuable time and money but I realise that not every couple either wants or can afford to hire someone. Myself and many colleagues will offer a complimentary phone consultation when we can advise, answer questions and get you on track.

Boring as it might seem, the key really is to know exactly what you can afford to spend, then decide how much you actually want to spend (the two amounts may be quite different) and create **a Budget** to work with. This will give you a framework within which to work with a guideline as to how much you can afford to spend on each element and supplier. Every couple's priorities are different and some will choose to spend more on food and beverage whilst others will focus on the quality of their photography for example. For some people flowers are just not important whilst for others beautiful and creative floral arrangements will provide their centrepieces and WOW! factor.

should be the very first thing you work out as it will dictate how much you should spend on your venue and ceremony, your food and beverage options and how many guests you can invite to work within your Budget. Of course, you can tweak this as you wish – if you like a venue which is more than you really wanted to pay but includes some items that you would otherwise have to source as extras then this is a good thing or you can reduce down in another area to balance the figures back out.

I'm always surprised by the amount of couples who choose to ignore the experience and advice of seasoned professionals – whether that be florists, caterers, photographers, Wedding Planners or venues – preferring to go ahead and do their own thing often with disappointing or expensive consequences. Please don't let that be you. Always ask questions and Listen, Listen, Listen before you finalise your master plan.

---oOo---

'Back to Nature' - Inspiration for a Woodland Themed Wedding.

I always try to incorporate nature and the surroundings into my designs as much as possible, especially for Destination Weddings, when I will use sand, shells, wood, natural stone, brick or whatever's available. I'm also especially fond of incorporating trees into outdoor wedding settings where they can make wonderful natural canopies to shade from the sun or you can attach fabrics to create gorgeous sweeping canopies. Lanterns and lights hanging through the trees also bring a magical feel as the day turns into evening.

Photocredit: Wasing Woodland Weddings

Always try to let the outside flow in and vice versa with a gentle transition between spaces especially if the indoor space is cavernous or a bit dark. If you are hiring a marquee topiary works well just outside the door, maybe forming a walkway, and small trees and planters dotted around inside can enhance your layout. Naturalistic design can incorporate inspirations from anything in nature. Natural colours from the earth tones palette eg. browns, tans, greens, white and off-white can be set off with bold colourful accents or use of metallics. Use of twigs – either sprayed to achieve a certain colour or natural – can be used in your table centrepieces or in floor standing arrangements. You can wire lemons or wicker hearts onto these, depending upon your theme, and they work really well with any type of Rustic styling. Outdoor ceremony settings using haybales or tree trunks or chairs carved from wood and wooden arches will work well within this theme.

The use of any natural water eg. a fountain, lake, moat or pond and ruined walls or buildings create interest. Natural brickwork and stone, exposed timber, cobbled paving etc. can all be emphasised although I wouldn't advocate having all your finishes in the same material, break it up or add something ie. a wooden floor and a natural brick wall/ backdrop will need some foliage, colourful floral accents, tall candelabra and subtle lighting. How about using different textures for fabrics including cottons, linen, jute, raffia etc. and go strong with your napkins, table runners or chairbacks. Can you feel how cosy and welcoming that space would be? Then you can go on to add in your tables, chairs and finishing touches.

---oOo---

Top Tips for Planning Your Wedding from Luxury Wedding Planner Kerry Jackson-Rider.

Planning a wedding can be the most magical time of your relationship, it is the romantic and special time in which you and your partner get to spend time preparing a wonderful event in which to celebrate your love in front of your friends and family. But if you're busy working, running a family or with other things it can also be difficult to know where to start.

The **Sanyukta Shrestha, London team** know how helpful a **little expert advice** can be so we called on **Kerry Jackson-Rider, luxury London wedding planner**, to give you some **tops tips for your wedding planning.**

What is the first thing that you suggest brides to be organise? I always suggest the couple decide which type of **wedding ceremony** they would like first of all and then choose a couple of dates which they prefer. They can then check availability with their preferred venues, arrange a visit and provisionally book one and then the other before confirming.

How long do you suggest couples leave to plan a wedding? 12 months is the perceived normal requirement for**wedding planning** although I find some couples, who perhaps would like to save up a bit more money, can start their planning 18 months to two years in advance. I also have clients who get engaged and decide to get married as soon as possible for various reasons, which can be from 4 weeks – 6 months. I call this a 'whirlwind wedding' and I really like these as the short time-frame means that momentum is kept up and decisions are made quickly.

You specialise in organising destination weddings, what is the first piece of advice you would give to a couple looking to plan a wedding abroad but unsure where to start? If a couple are unsure I would always advise them to fully consider all the factors i.e. Why do they feel a destination wedding would meet their needs; what is their available budget; what time of year are they considering and what potential location; what are their guest numbers and logistics. Quite often, after careful consideration of their personal requirements, even though it sounds idyllic and romantic, a couple will decide that a destination wedding is not right for them.

Image source : www.kerryjackson-rider.co.uk

What is the easiest way to create a budget plan? By using a spreadsheet. Even if you are not very technical and don't use the formulas a spreadsheet is a neat, organised way to keep your estimated and actual costs in check and also serves as a useful tool for working through your planning.

How do you recommend brides keep a track of their wedding plans? The spreadsheet idea works very well as an overview and you can see who you have got quotes in from, when you have paid a deposit etc. A regular A4 file with dividers and plastic sleeves also keeps everything in good order. I know some Brides2B like to buy planners to record dates and collect pictures, colour swatches etc. and, of course, Pinterest is now a super techie way of producing design boards and it's also great fun! I also give all my couples a '**Wedding Countdown'** which we check against every time we meet up. This way they can actually see the progress being made and it makes them happy to know everything is on track.

When would you recommend brides begin to wedding dress shop? A lot of brides surprise me by buying their dresses very quickly. I would always recommend that you wait, at least until you know your venue and style, as sometimes the two don't quite match up to your expectation. I have known brides who have actually bought new dresses before the wedding as they decided they no longer liked their original impulse buy.

When would you recommend that brides organise flowers, décor and invitations? It all depends on the time-frame to your wedding day but certainly **Save the Dates** should be sent out asap especially if you are having a **Destination Wedding** as your guests also need time to book holiday from work etc. When sending invitations you need to take into consideration any holidays eg. Christmas/ Summer and allow extra time for people to respond. Also, remember that you are looking to receive your **guests' RSVPs** at least 8 weeks before the wedding date. You can begin to plan your flowers and décor once your venues are confirmed.

When is the best time to arrange hair trials, make up trials etc? At least **3 months before the wedding** so that you have time to grow your hair and get it in top condition and also begin a beauty regime all on personal advice received from your chosen **hair and make up artists**.

What should brides consider when looking for a photographer? Most importantly, you should consider your **wedding style**, **your budget** and **what you want to achieve from the photography**. Then look at the work of several photographers online, if you don't already have a favourite, to see whose style of photography resonates with you. Then you can make appointments with no more than 3 to meet with them and discuss your requirements. See how you feel in their company. Are you comfortable with them? Ask if they will **offer a pre-wedding shoot/ get to know you session**; if you are looking for an album or printed materials ask to see some samples; double check what is included in their quote and don't forget that travel expenses may be extra. You should book your chosen photographer asap to avoid disappointment.

Would you recommend live entertainment on the big day? Definitely! As many varieties as you can afford within your budget. Nothing creates atmosphere like a **live band** although many couples like to have a **DJ** as well. It works well to split the evening into segments taking into account who will provide the soundtrack to your first dance. A close up magician or caricaturist and a children's entertainer will entertain your guests and avoid any lull in the proceedings.

Bridal showers a do or a don't? I think a bridal shower or hen party provides a nice opportunity for the bride to get together with her female friends and relatives for a bit of girly fun. So, yes I'm all for it!

What legal documentation should couples consider and at what point in wedding planning? Once you've decided**what type of wedding ceremony** you would like to have, and where, you can begin to make the arrangements. **A registrar's office** will make you an appointment to give notice and provide you with all the information you need. For a**church wedding** you will need to make an appointment with your **vicar or priest** to check availability of your preferred date and to start the wedding process. For a Catholic wedding abroad you will need to gain permission from your local priest before you can arrange this. If you choose to have a Destination Wedding I cannot stress strongly enough that consideration of the legal requirements of the country which you are considering as a potential location is **very important** and should be looked into straight away as part of your initial research as is the legality of the marriage in your own country. Visas and inoculations are also important considerations. The legal aspect is often what makes planning a destination wedding seem more complicated but, as long as you seek advice from the relevant authorities, it should not be a problem.

How can weddings be made more personal? Weddings should be totally personalised to the bride and groom. Wouldn't it be awful if they were all the same as if they had come off a conveyor belt ...? **Every wedding should be influenced by the couple's individual style, their personalities, their hobbies, their wedding vision, their budget, their chosen venues, the season, their guests** etc etc. How can a wedding not be uniquely personal?!?

How can a couple show their wedding party their appreciation in a personal and unique way? I encourage my couples to try to 'surprise' their guests as much as possible within the ceremony and reception and this can involve many ideas both expensive and non-expensive. Again, it is easy to reflect the couple's personality and the special relationships that they have with different groups on the guest list ie. close friends, siblings, older family members. Favours is another way of showing appreciation and, again, I encourage my couples to consider very thoughtfully what they present and how.

How can you ensure the couple and guests have a unique experience? By tailoring the day to their exact requirements, by getting to know them and what they like and dislike, by listening and observing and by adding my own 'unique touches'. I also like to surprise the bride and groom whilst they are surprising their guests!

Romantic setting, Image: from Pinterest

Are there any must haves that brides should remember on the big day? Most brides are very traditional at heart and many like to follow the rhyme, **"Something old, something new, something borrowed, something blue (and a silver sixpence for my shoe)"** and they tend to collect things from friends and family members in line with this, which is very sweet and means a lot, especially to grandmother's, aunts and mums. I don't think brides should carry a bag but certainly their important bits and pieces including tissues, lipstick, any medication etc. should be kept handy by the Maid of Honour. A wedding planner, when used, will pop the brides personal items into her '**Emergency Kit**' which will be close by for all eventualities.

What would you say is the most important thing to remember on the big day? To have fun and enjoy yourself. The day goes by so quickly, I always tell my couples to enjoy the company of their friends and family, to take a few snatched moments to enjoy each other's company and to really try to soak up the atmosphere. This is one of the reasons a**videographer** is worth their weight in gold as they can capture the atmosphere and moments the bride and groom might miss yet they can watch the video over and over again and enjoy a different new experience each time.

Benefits of a wedding planner
Why would you recommend a wedding planner? If you can afford it and you would like professional help then I think you should go for it. The Benefits of using a wedding planner will always far outweigh the perceived cost and is truly your investment in achieving the wedding of your dreams.

What packages do most planners offer? Most wedding planners will offer a range of services from 'On the Day Co-ordination, through various 'Partial Planning' packages to a 'Full Wedding Planning' service. The price of these services ranges quite considerably and is very much time related eg. the normal conventions are 40 hours for 'On the Day' and 250 hours for' Full Planning'. 'Partial Planning' packages are usually from 4wks before, 3 months before and 6 months before the wedding date.

If brides take on a wedding planner how often should they expect to meet with a planner?

How involved can brides and couples to be in the planning process if they choose a wedding planner? All wedding planners will differ in the amount of contact time they are able to offer their clients. Since fees are very much time related, in theory, the less a wedding planner charges for a service the less time they will have available to spend with a client. Since I only offer a luxury 'Full Wedding Planning' service my clients have unlimited email and telephone access to me 24/7 whilst we are planning their wedding and we have regular meetings depending upon the time-frame of the wedding and subject to my and their own availability. Couples should be as involved in their wedding planning as they wish and since a lot of clients are busy professionals who often work abroad or spend periods of time overseas, using the services of a wedding planner means that, once they know their 'vision' is in a safe pair of hands, they can relax and not only enjoy their engagement but also carry on with their work and social lives which is important for them.

---oOo---

Daily Express Game of Thrones article.

A Medieval banquet, queens and wenches: How to throw a Game Of Thrones-style wedding.
HAVING a white wedding is so last year! Themed nuptials are now in vogue and what better way to celebrate your big day than with a lavish ceremony inspired by hit fantasy series Game Of Thrones?

Themed weddings are becoming more and more popular. Throw a Star Trek inspired ceremony, dress up as Barbie and Ken for your nuptials or get your granny to dress up as catwoman for a superhero style bash. The possibilities are endless.

Last September, Napster co-founder and first Facebook president Sean Parker celebrated his marriage like a king in a magnificent and extravagant Medieval themed wedding.

Inspired, and just weeks away from the fourth season of gripping Medieval fantasy series Game Of Thrones, we spoke to London-based luxury wedding planner Kerry Jackson-Rider to find out how to create the perfect Game of Thrones big day (but without the bloodshed usually associated with Westeros nuptials).

From frocks to flowers there are many ways of making your perfect day fit for a king and queen.

A dungeon, castle or cellar is the perfect location for a Game Of T
VENUE: Create your own banquet hall

Finding the perfect venue is key. A dungeon, castle or cellar with stone floors, walls and a vaulted ceiling is ideal.

Create the right ambience through clever use of lighting with fire baskets, fire torches and lanterns. Use lots of gothic-style metal for thrones and chairs, draped with furs or fabrics and large floor standing vases and candelabra.

Aim to make everything "larger than life" and create an awe-inspiring but fun and comfortable setting for you and your guests to enjoy. If you can get hold of some real or imitation snow and a dragon ice sculpture you will be well on your way.

Add some long wooden tables and benches for the wedding breakfast and full size trees or twigs either natural or sprayed white or silver. For your altar a big stone table carved with gargoyles or dragons would look fantastic.

DRESS CODE: Flowing robes for all

Ask your guests to dress up but do give them some guidelines. Clothing should consist of be free flowing robes, leggings in dark and royal colours, crowns or head dresses, along with accessories and large jewellery.

Hairstyles are usually long, wavy and natural looking. Furs, boots, belts, cloaks, velvet and metallic braid embellishments could be used both in the ladies' hair and at the waist.

FOOD: A feast of meat and mead

Try a banquet setting with a long top table and long tables leading up to it. Table settings should be rustic, using good quality items such as candles, large fruit bowls, bunches of grapes, and platters of food boards for sharing.

Use pewter tableware and glasses for your "mead" and ask servers and waiters to dress as "wenches."

A signature wedding cake should be carried in shoulder high by four men to create a spectacle. The cake should be in bold colours and decorated with emblems like a coat of arms.

The couple could create their own coat of arms and use this also for banners and flags to be set at the entrance.

The cake should be an unusual shape, not a regular round three tier, so possibly square or oblong with at least three quarters of the tiers of different shapes and sizes.

Dark red, deep purple and blossom coloured flowers make a dramatic **ENTERTAINMENT: Ye**

olde minstrels

Have a myriad of entertainers performing in short bursts while the guests are seated, such as a snake charmer, juggler, fire eater and stilt walkers.

Go over the top and be surprising to create the wow factor. Minstrels and acrobats get guests off their seats in order to start the party and a live band will keep it going until the small hours.

FLOWERS: Choose rustic blooms

Create the bride's bouquet with simple, meadow-style flowers, such as daisies, bluebells and dandelion, and decorate with twigs, follage and leaves.

Bridesmaids can carry small posies with follage in a contrasting coloured flower and have flowers in their hair.

TRANSPORT: Leave your car at home

Horses and wooden carts, of course!

---oOo---

Getting Married in the UK vs. a Romantic and Affordable Destination Wedding.
The Soaring Cost of Getting Married in the UK vs. a Romantic and Affordable Destination Wedding/

Honeymoon as featured on Wedding Magazine online athttp://www.weddingmagazine.co.uk/blog/?p=2479

With the recently announced 40% rise in fees for Church of England weddings from £295 to £415 from January 2013 many couples must be wondering if there is a cheaper option. This is the basic cost of getting married in church and covers the reading of the banns and a certificate. Extras, many of which most couples will want, including the verger, heating, the choir, organ, bells and flowers will bring the cost up to £1000 plus. Keeping our eye on just the basic cost of getting married in church, this is still relatively good compared to Civil wedding ceremonies where the current basic cost can range from £140.50 to £510.50 depending upon your chosen venue. Who's to say that these prices won't also increase in the near future but, currently, the cheapest way to get married is in the Register Office from Monday to Saturday and the most expensive way is to get married at an approved venue on a Sunday or Bank Hollday. Of course, to the Registrar's fees you must also add any hire charges for your chosen venue, possibly a stately home or hotel, which can range from £300 to £3000, although they will often waive this dependent upon the type of venue, your guest numbers and your reception arrangements.

So, given that the average cost of a wedding in the UK is currently £21,500 and with a marquee wedding starting from £25,000 and a lavish wedding costing in the region of £100,000 it is not, financially, a venture to be entered into lightly. What do you really get for your money? If you think about it, it's the deposit for a nice house and you could certainly have a couple of very nice holidays and some change left over.

This is why more and more couples (26% last year alone) are choosing a Destination Wedding. You can have an amazing time abroad for this amount of money and I will tell you why… choice and affordability! The only down side, that I can think of, is if you hate travelling in particular flying.

Weddings at home mean many couples end up having to invite everyone because they can. The fact is that guests = expense. The more guests you invite the more expensive your wedding will become. Couples who choose to have a Destination Wedding often actually do so because they want to go on their own or have a small, intimate affair with just their closest friends and family. Even for larger gatherings, often with guests arriving from all around the world, the comparative cost vs. a home wedding makes it a no brainer. For some couples though the idea of some of their special guests being unable to travel (ie. elderly or pregnant relations, small children and babies) does deter them from doing what they really want to do. Also, sometimes the issue of should you pay for all your guests or ask them to pay for their own flights/ accommodation is often a key deciding factor depending upon budget and the couple's priorities. You must decide what you truly want to do and, if you choose to take only a handful of people or stipulate a 'no children' policy then that is your choice. If you do decide to go on your own, two witnesses can easily be provided for you, and you can arrange a special celebration party when you get back. Then you get the best of both worlds! If you decide to invite lots of guests you can turn your wedding into a holiday of 7-14 days or a long weekend, depending on location, and enjoy at least 3-4 special days with family and friends.

There are so many amazing choices of venue for your wedding ceremony and reception overseas – beaches, vineyards, castles, mountain retreats, jungle hideaways, game lodges etc. Also the weather is sure to make for an idyllic celebration. Naturally some destinations are more suitable than others at different times of the year. Many of the best loved choices may be too hot or too wet at the time you would like to get married. If possible, choose your destination first then tie in your date or, if you choose a special date first, be sure to check out prices and climate to find the best destination for you at that time. Here is an overview of just a few overseas destinations which will certainly provide you with better value for money, more choice and an even more romantic, truly memorable wedding experience than you ever dreamed possible.

Photocredit: Twelve Apostles Hotel

South Africa for example. It is not only very romantic, it is also very affordable! You can get married in a beautiful ceremony then go on honeymoon for two weeks and the cost will still be much lower than getting married in the UK! Unlike many other popular destinations, in South Africa, there is no legal requirement for residency prior to the wedding although arrival a few days before is advisable. You CAN get married outside and on the beach (although signing of the register must take place inside after the ceremony). There is NO restriction on day or time meaning you can get married on any day of the week at any time! South Africa is so ideal for a Weddingmoon – a combined wedding and honeymoon – in just two weeks you can explore and see so many things. The weather is glorious all year round but two beautiful months to visit South Africa for your wedding are in April (when Autumn starts and the heat of Summer is bearable) and in September (when Spring brings the first greenery and amazing cloud formations while the cold Winter weather is over). A civil ceremony will cost in the region of £1000 although £6000 should be enough for a wonderful celebration with family and friends.

Beautiful and exotic, Zanzibar, 'the spice island' lies just 35km off the coast of Tanzania in the Indian Ocean. You can also combine your visit to Zanzibar with a mini Safari in Tanzania or Kenya choosing from a selection of safari locations and accommodation types. Weddings on Zanzibar are legally recognised and you can enjoy either a religious ceremony in a church or a civil ceremony on the beach, in a garden or at a hotel usually around 4/5pm when it is cooler. Your ceremony can also include a romantic sunset dhow cruise. Legal requirements are quite straightforward in that you must be on Zanzibar for four working days before your ceremony. All the little extras which will make your Wedding on Zanzibar special and unique are often included or else very affordable – for example, exotic tropical flowers for your bouquet, buttonholes and floral arches, a candlelit dinner for two on the beach (often included as a gift by your resort), a sunset dhow cruise, your cake, your photographer, musicians and dancers, hair and make up artists and Masai warriors who will form a guard of honour for you! The cost of an officiant is £270 but is included in one resort's inclusive pricing, which ranges from £1461 – 1618, or within another's pricing of £32 per head (£3200 for a fully catered reception for 100 guests) which also includes everything else you could possibly need to make your celebration amazing. Where would you got all that in the UK?

Photocredit: Virginie Faucher

Marrakech in Morocco is a great choice for your Destination Wedding being only a 3 hour flight away from the UK and is truly exotic and romantic. It also has all-year round sunshine (although March to May and September to November are the optimum times for your wedding) and is ideal both for a small, intimate Wedding or for larger celebrations with family and friends. It is possible to enjoy a truly magical celebration in Marrakech because it is close to home and so affordable to arrange it is much easier for couples to invite more guests than they would be able, say, to a wedding in The Caribbean or Thailand where travel and accommodation costs might be too high. What makes a wedding in Marrakech extra special are the romantic extras readily available and affordable such as camels, Berber tents, rose petals everywhere, palm trees, fountains, dancers, musicians and much much more. A lavish, fully catered, three day affair in a beautiful and exclusive venue in 'La Palmeraie' with entertainment and everything you could wish for can be achieved for £45,000 whilst a more low key celebration, again for three days, in a riad can cost as little as £4000. Morocco is one of the destinations where it is not currently possible to have a legally recognised Civil wedding, so this would take place in the UK with a blessing, religious wedding or a traditional Moroccan wedding ceremony taking place in Marrakech. An English style wedding can be performed by a celebrant and a wedding or blessing may be held in the Catholic Church of Marrakech. A ceremony and reception which includes traditional Moroccan wedding finishing touches will provide a wonderful and colourful spectacle which you and your guests will remember for ever.

A luxury, all inclusive 'Beautiful Beginnings'

wedding at one of Sandals' 13 Caribbean resorts can be free if you stay for six nights or longer, otherwise it will cost only £222 and will provide you with better value for your money and a wonderful couples' experience. You can choose another of Martha Stewart's exclusive themes for your wedding with a price range from £1015 – £3806.

Our own exclusive and luxurious 'Heaven on Earth' wedding experience in Halkidiki, Greece can be enjoyed from just £25,000 and includes the most incredible suites and idyllic location in The Aegean not to mention fine dining, the best wines and champagnes, world class spa treatments and the ultimate in pampering and romance. Although included, the comparative civil ceremony fee at the local town hall in Hanioti would be just £209.

So, undoubtedly by choosing to have a Destination Wedding you will get more for your money and more choice. With costs per head working out at much less for much more received and with the added benefits of sun, sea, a bit of adventure and a holiday all rolled into one it really is a great way to throw a party for your family and friends which you and they will treasure and remember forever without you having to spend a fortune.

---oOo---

How to Plan a Wedding in 10 Weeks: 'Whirlwind Weddings' article in Conde Nast Brides Magazine.

I was delighted to be asked to write this article on **'Whirlwind Weddings'** for Conde Nast Brides Magazine which they have now featured online and in their Newsletter. It came about following the celebrity engagement of Marvin (JLS) and Rochelle (The Saturdays) and the fact that they have said they want to get married by the end of March 2012! Yes, it is less than 10 weeks! I hope you find it helpful if you are planning your wedding in a short time. If you find you need some help or advice please do give me a call.

How to Plan a Wedding in 10 Weeks:

Planning a wedding can be stressful at the best of times – but what if you have to squeeze months and months of work in to just a few weeks? We asked **Luxury Wedding Planner Kerry Jackson-Rider** who specialises in this area for her advice:

Is it possible to fit months and months of planning into just a matter of weeks?

"Of course it is! All you need is lots of free time and the ability to make fast and informed decisions, quite often on the spot. The quickest wedding I know of was planned in just 3 weeks but expect to be spending practically all your waking hours on it. This is why it would be a good idea to have a good wedding planner by your side to help."

So where do we start?

"First things to decide are what type of ceremony you want and where ie. religious or civil, home or destination. Don't forget that many popular destinations have legal and residency requirements to take into consideration. Next you can begin to think about the venue and number of guests. The biggest problem with giving your guests short notice is definitely making travel arrangements, especially for overseas guests; getting a 'Save the Date' or, if possible, your invitations out ASAP is vital.

Another problem you may encounter is not being able to get your first choice venue and, indecd, your favourite suppliers. Out of season is going to be a lot easier BUT you need to be prepared for this and definitely have a Plan B."

What about the dress?

"You're not going to have the normal amount of lead in time to order that designer dress. You may have to buy off the peg or look out for some incredible sample sales which can include one-off prototypes by top designers."

So what are the Top 10 Things to Do?

1. Decide upon date
2. Type of ceremony
3. Preferred location/ venue
4. Guest list and numbers

5. Guests' travel arrangements

6. Save the Date/ Invitations out ASAP
7. Book ceremony and reception venues
8. Book suppliers – photographer, catering,

entertainment, flowers, transport, hair and make up, any extras
9. Attire/ rings/ accessories
10. Book honeymoon

There are many other things you may or may not like to schedule in too eg. gift list, hair and make up trials, seating plan, passport and vaccinations, menu tasting, wedding cake, hen and stag parties, writing vows and speeches. It may all sound a bit overwhelming which is why you need to be VERY organised and focused or **hire a wedding planner** who has the experience and the contacts on speed dial to provide you with great service and worth.

Sounds very stressful, do you have any words of advice?
"I personally think that planning a wedding in a short amount of time is very exciting as you have to keep the momentum going and it builds very quickly towards the big day. I also think, for some reason – probably the extreme focus, that it is easier to gel everything together. When you are working on a wedding for 12 – 18 months, ie. when you have loads more time, I find couples regularly change their minds about things, which is only natural. It is a good option because you can spread everything out, especially payments, and there is no rush. Some couples love this but others I know have felt that it was way too long a process and wished they'd got married a lot more quickly. The great thing is, whichever your preference, that every couples' wedding ideas and timeframes are so different which is what makes every wedding unique and a joy to help create. Remember all things are possible!"

Kerry Jackson-Rider

9 ABOUT THE AUTHOR.

Kerry Jackson-Rider is the founder and owner of Kerry Jackson-Rider Luxury Wedding Planning and is a leading International Wedding Planner and Designer. With over 10 years experience in Wedding and Event Planning, Kerry 'custom designs' every wedding and event with a unique brand of stylish elegance and attention to detail whether in London, the UK or around the world. She never fails to bring creativity to your unique event. She will take your vision and create an unforgettably stylish Destination Wedding in elegant Paris, exotic Marrakech or on a romantic beach in Thailand working, as she does, across the world.

Kerry also manages wedding venues for prestigious clients, runs 'exclusive' Wedding Planner Training & Mentoring programmes worldwide, is a guest lecturer at The University of East London and is extremely proud to be a Mentor with The Branson Centre of Entrepreneurship Caribbean. For media, article and speaking requests please contact the office on Tel: +44 (0)7860 580794 or email hello@kerryjacksonrider.co.uk .

You can visit the website at
www.kerryjacksonrider.co.uk

Skype address: kerryjackson-rider

Follow Kerry for great ideas and inspiration on:

Twitter:
www.Twitter.com/@Kerry_weddings
Pinterest:
http://pinterest.com/LuxuryWedding
Facebook:
www.facebook.com/KerryJacksonRiderL
uxuryWeddingPlanning
Blog:
http://www.kerryjacksonrider.co.uk/blog

Printed in Great Britain
by Amazon.co.uk, Ltd.,
Marston Gate.